For Gillian, Kate and Jack

Some of these poems have appeared in *Poetry & All That Jazz, South, The Interpreter's House, The Frogmore Papers, Monkey Kettle, Heatwave, the Morning Star,* and *The New European;* online at *Ink, Sweat and Tears, Algebra of Owls, The Screech Owl, I Am Not A Silent Poet, Places of Poetry,* and *Poetry in Surrey Libraries;* and in Dempsey & Windle's *What Next?,* Kingston University competition *Short Cuts,* and *Stairwell Press' York* anthologies.

CONTENTS

THE FLOWERPOT MEN

We were born in the same year
at the dawn of the brave new Elizabethan era.
Men-children fussed over by Little Weed,
often collapsing at their own jokes,
pots rattling, cackling, guffawing,

The strange figure with squeaky voice
they occasionally met in the wood gave
me nightmares. Growing older
we smirked at the druggy connotations.
I saw them as dazed, strung-out, crawling

out of their horticultural crash pads after bad trips
or hangovers. Hanging loose. Some people
had no time for their games, nonsense talk;
maybe it was just a blokey thing.
They cavorted while the God-like, unseen man

who worked in their garden of Eden
took his lunch break. But did He,
like the Little House, know everything?
Everyone remembers a Bill and Ben.
Perhaps all those benders caught up with them.

THE OAK TREE

A misshapen old man
that barred our way to school.
We would sidle past,
caps over our eyes,
the aged oak in Greenfield Avenue,
so wide the path went round it;
startling, lurid growths
in its crevices,
crumbling at a touch.

Aware of beauty, we gathered
cobwebs, glistening with dew
and sunlight, netting them
as gleaming fish in rock pools,
with bent twigs. In those days
we still saw hedgehogs,
they weren't unusual, bumbling
along in front of our footsteps,
or curled up, defying calamity.

FREE SCHOOL MILK

My first job. How I loved it,
maybe more than any other.
Carting crates of milk from class
to class. My gang of mates.
Returning for the empties,
bottles clinking, metal clanging.

Third of a pint for everyone.
Girls often left some.
The leftover milk smelt funny,
but I knocked it back.
Blokes going about their business,
full of purpose, learning

something, camaraderie,
teamwork, building muscles.
You needed strength
to lift those crates.
I can't recall the name, but
some killjoy put a stop to all that.

MARPLES MUST GO!

Slogan daubed on a motorway bridge
in the Sixties, left there
for decades for generations
of football fans and musicians
to wonder at on their way north.

A peculiar transport minister
more to blame than Beeching
for the vandalism of the railways.
He had a pecuniary interest in motorways,
a finger in the pie, you might say.

There was Profumo, but few knew
at the time that Ernie had a fetish
for dressing up in women's clothes
and being chastised. He richly
deserved every stroke of the lash.

The M1 peters out north of Leeds,
merges with the A1, a much older road
(turn left for Barnard Castle,
if you can read the signs).
Marples Must Go! And go he did,

after getting his peerage, flitting
on the night ferry to Monaco
to escape a huge tax bill. He's history,
just another perverse politician
putting his foot down on our road to ruin.

SPACE PATROL

Forget Fireball XL5, Thunderbirds,
or Captain Scarlet. Remember Venusian Slim,
Martian Husky, and Captain Larry Dart,
a Democrat-voting Charlton Heston,
with goatee. Diverse crew long
before Star Trek. You'd find them
checking out the rings of Saturn,
swamps of Jupiter, going into the freezer,
leaving things to the robots.

Ethereal B-movie avant-garde music.
The Gabblerdictum was a kind
of Martian parrot. Beautiful Marla at HQ:
A Venusian has the facility never to forget.
All aboard the Galasphere!
All in order, captain. I'm ready.
Yobba rays were Husky's department:
All I want's a Martian sausage,
delivered in an eastern European accent.

BERRYLANDS

An apology for a station
on the way to Hampton Court,
the place where the fast
slowed down for Surbiton.
It overlooked a sewage farm
we'd cycle past, a short cut.
Lower Marsh Lane
more or less summed it up.

Sad? Not for us.
John and I would trainspot there,
watching the Merchant Navies
and Battle of Britains
round the bend and thunder
towards us, while listening
to the cricket, our conquerors
Worrell and Sobers, Hall and Griffiths.

Days that vanished in a puff of smoke.
But now smellylands is in the news,
a "cannabis forest" found
on waste ground
close to the effluent,
growing under the noses
of police and residents
more used to the whiff of sewage.

Commuters may have seen the plants
as they looked blearily out of the window.
Police said it resembled
a forest of Christmas trees.
Sensibilities and scents of outrage.
something in the water.
As a university acquaintance once said to me:
This is bloody good shit, mate.

'SUBTERRANEAN HOMESICK BLUES' ON JUKE BOX JURY

BBC trying to get with the Sixties.
After this strange-sounding single
was played compere David Jacobs
repeated the title in his
suave Light Programme voice
and only just the hint of a sneer.

The panel – people like
Eartha Kitt and Pete Murray –
looked at each other, trying
not to laugh. The last thing
they wanted was to seem square.
They had pretended to get the Beatles

and those other long-haired groups.
But this jangling clattering
concoction of words, like a box
of spanners being shaken?
This was too much, would never
catch on. Jacobs pressed his buzzer.

It reached number nine.
And I've remembered
something else;
a character called
Mr Jones was there.

THE WEEKEND STARTS HERE

Mick shrugging off the half-hearted teenagers
told by the director to get up on stage
and grab him; concentrating more
on his moves than his miming,
holding it all back on Little Red Rooster.

Cilla's face lit with wide-eyed astonishment
that all this really was happening.
Sixteen-year-old Lulu
descending a staircase
knowing exactly what was happening.

Them, led by him. The Beach Boys
in their striped shirts; strangely,
not very hip at all. Gerry crossing
the Mersey; the robotic Dave Clark Five;
a lost and left behind Billy Fury.

Dusty at her happiest
in her Motown comfort zone
trying too hard to transmit her joy.
Martha and the Vandellas,
Heatwave in all its glory.

SUMMER CAMP

We trudged through woods
on Porlock hill when Nobby Stiles
was dancing at Wembley. That
summer camp it didn't stop raining,

resulting in the great latrine disaster,
the trench giving way
while someone was astride it.
The memory of his roar of distress

still makes me laugh, unaccountably.
The thrill of wide games after dark
when all the lights went out.
Scouting for Boers:

Wash your parts in cold water
and cool them down.
Sound advice, if you can, I suppose.
But *avoid rich food, too much meat*?

I never made patrol leader,
couldn't fathom the knots.
Career pattern established
at an early age. My final act before

leaving the Scouts was to quit
my disintegrating bivouac
and retreat back to camp.
Next summer I swore

would be different. It was.
To my great surprise I found
myself in a caravan one
Saturday night sprawled on a bed

with a blonde from Swansea.
Character-forming? Maybe.
But what kind of character?
Glad I didn't try climbing mountains.

I wasn't much cop at the practical stuff.

DUSTY ON THE DANSETTE

It wasn't a soft-porn movie.
But yes, she was a Danish au pair
in my Methodist nana's front parlour
while Dusty's Son of a Preacher Man
played on the Dansette.

Miniskirt, boots; first, necessarily
brief but genuine encounter. Ah,
but she had a bit of a cold
that night. Inexpert as I was,
I could tell she was just being polite,

that her heart wasn't in it. Our tryst
ended when she blew her nose loudly.
Sometimes I remember when I hear
the song. I'm a big Dusty fan. But
Aretha's version is superior, I have to admit.

THE GRAMMAR SCHOOL

He turned up pissed, fresh
from the pub: glazed face,
breathing beer, gazed at the boy
in the front desk, stroked
his blond shock of hair.
It was all such a hoot.
About him flew books,
duffel bags, hockey boots.

The ale wore off, he growled
for quiet; clutched
with nicotine fingers the Penguin
Book of Contemporary Verse,
decades out of date.
He coughed and choked,
forgot where he was.
He read with passion,

youth and tears: Hardy,
Owen, Larkin, Hughes.
Some still chucked stuff,
guffawed uneasily.
But listen. If anyone asks,
if there was one teacher …
His lesson was this:
bards, booze, cigs and blues.

CROSSING THE ROAD

Everyone is distracted by the cover,
the zebra crossing walk,
Lennon already dressed by Yoko
in unimpeachable white,
McCartney barefoot, out of step,
therefore dead. And the name,
the famous studios where they
and George Martin mixed up magic.

The penultimate album released
but the last one they recorded.
Glorious long medley on side two,
a cluster of daft characters,
and half-finished songs,
sum greater than the segments.
The fans unaware of the arguments
but fearing that something was wrong.

The dream was over: final
gasp of the British empire.
England wouldn't swing any more.
Hello, goodbye, you fab four.

DUST-UP IN LEAMINGTON

Did we somehow know the score?
How could we? We were only students,
mostly. Five hundred outside
the gates on a November night
when the 'Milk Snatcher, Union Basher'
came to speak at a Leamington
girls school's speech day.

Union basher? Some small measure
that the education minister
had taken against students,
hardly an augury.
Milk snatcher? She'd cancelled
the schoolkids' free milk as well.
That should have been the warning.

New kid, arriving early for my first demo,
I was close to the police line
that buckled when the Bristol Young Trotskyists
shouted and heaved. Half a dozen
found ourselves on the other side.
One ran madly towards the school.
I stood there, awaiting punishment.

A police sergeant hurled me headfirst
into the crowd. A housemate dusted
me down: *Don't worry. I spat in his eye.*
Saw him wiping it away.
I nodded and laughed,
but felt sorry for the sergeant,
and wondered when he'd get his tea.

CHUCK BERRY'S DING-A-LING

Halfway through the year I knew
I wouldn't make the grade.
A freezing night in '72,
the time of Bloody Sunday.
Tension in Coventry.
But rock and roll
can save your soul.
Johnny B Goode,
lift me from my misery.

I had nowhere else to go.
The duck walk, Nadine, Carol,
Maybelline, and the novelty
song that must have
eaten half the set. A wolfish grin,
part-shaman, part-showman.
We bellowed as Chuck
gleefully short-changed us.
The joke was they recorded it.

Months later top of the charts,
hundreds of us on the vinyl.
Number one, ma, that's me!
By then I'd dropped out.
But I'd danced out of the Locarno
at midnight, past housemates
queuing to see the Floyd.
The night that was
the start of my comeback.

ANDY WILLIAMS

When I was young I didn't get it:
the crooning, whining, almost girlish voice.
Middle of the road, hope I die before I get that old.
Music my girlfriend's parents danced to,
waltzing with stern expressions and stiff backs.

Thirty years later, watching them
still dancing I thought,
if we could only move like that.
Wouldn't it be wonderful?

And then I understood.
Andy Williams, the king
of cool, whispering in ears
the persuasive sounds
of swinging, middle-aged sex.

THE LOCAL RAG

Sniff those yesteryear newspapers;
damp romantic whiff of the local rag.
Crashing typewriters bashing
out wedding details, film previews,
match reports. Telephones
shrill with complaints, demands,
rare tip-offs. Deadline past,
the *petit mort* of the newsroom
on press day: the café that purveyed
fried egg sandwiches next door.

The snapper leered through his viewfinder;
young reporter yearning to be initiated
by the divorcee in ads. Potential for
murder mystery: lethal-looking spikes,
repository of handouts, rejected copy.
Ex-Fleet Street editor back from the pub,
bellowing arias as he laboured upstairs,
yearning for a scoop he could flog
to the nationals, looking for love,
loyalty and the next front-page lead.

[Postscript: the best of times didn't last,
premises acquired by an outlet selling burgers.
Cub reporter and spare-time metal detector
made his name with local histories.
Two thought estate agent a better career.
Another turned his hand to fixing chairs.
One went north, returned south to the Street,
before turning to poetry. Snapper seduced
by glamour photography now helps souls
off the street, in the name of the Saviour.]

THE ROAD NORTH

That tinderbox summer: subversive
underground fires breaking cover,
crackling heaths and pinewoods.
Blackened commons, smoke-cloaked motorway.
Sudden, meaningful quarrels; soon
you'd be heading north to university.

Fog-stalled autumn: drinks half-price
in freshers' week, tempted by new flavours.
Down south I couldn't start, awaited repairs.
Long, cross-country trips on stopping trains.
Returning late to a disapproving roommate;
something jeopardised, something gained.

Winter's tale: clinging scent of the sugar factory,
ancient streets loaded with history
and pubs. My kinda town. Sneaking out of your room
before the cleaners came in. Year of the Cat
on the jukebox in the bus station bar.
Waiting for the overnight coach back south,

certain I'd soon be heading north for good,
job in the offing. I'd tracked you down.

CYCLE STREET

Felt like we were playing house.
The little cul-de-sac off the main road,
end of terrace, front door on to the street.

Mischief nights. The kids knocking,
begging your Halloween pumpkin,
nipping in through the rear window
while our backs were turned.

The off-licence on the corner, the parties:
Graham Parker, Stranglers, Specials.
The back alleys where after three years
we knew someone was watching us.

Manuscripts coming back after two weeks.
My ensuing Do Not Disturbs.
Travelling from that cathedral of a station
to Scarborough and tea with your Nana,

back for the evening film on campus.
Cycling across town through Bootham Bar
to drink with the press gang. Our bed
for months just a mattress on the floor.

O, we were young and carefree there.

THE BATTLE OF HASTINGS, AS SUMMARISED BY ROY KEANE

Look at it not so much as a game
of two halves – although it was that,
too – but the result of fixture congestion.
Pure and simple. Two crucial matches,
far too close together. A great win up north,
despite Tostig's last-minute transfer
to the other side. Then the rush south.

Even then, the game could have been won.
Tight defensive set-up worked well
up to the break. It was a good plan,
if only they'd stuck to it. But they got
carried away, thought the Normans
were there for the taking, lost their shape,
got bogged down in midfield, left themselves

wide open at the back. Those tricky Normans
took full advantage. I don't blame the keeper,
he never saw it coming. But there was no need
to celebrate in that way. Everyone here at Sky
condemns the scenes that followed,
the repercussions of that defeat.
These foreigners coming over here

bringing in new rules. *Droit de seigenur*?
What's that all about? The bastards.
Excuse my French. It's the ordinary
fan I feel sorry for. I might get
into trouble for saying this, but October's
far too early in the season. No need
to dismember the manager, in my opinion.

27

WATCHING ENGLAND WITH
CAROL ANN DUFFY

It seems like a dream now:
the 1-4 scoreline;
Lampard's goal that never was;
watching the game with Carol Ann Duffy.

She turned up amid the half-time gloom
in the pub, asked if it was ok
to sit near the TV. I made some crack
about political-historical contexts
and Nazi fugitives, and why Uruguayan
officials might favour Germans.
She half-smiled: that's when I guessed.

The sort of joke you only make watching footie.
Sport and literature don't mix,
well, not in my book. But I peppered the goal
with witty apercus, thinking England's
laureate might write about the Three Lions
who had watched the match with her,
read it that night at the arts festival.

She didn't, of course. Although at one point
she did ask if Crouch had come on.
The referee blew. Did England's worst
World Cup finals beating mean
I should give up football for poetry?
The camera lingered on Capello, the tabloid target.
He should be carrying an umbrella, she said.

HOWAY THE LAD

It may be just a pre-season friendly,
he's the wrong side of thirty; I still
get the same joy watching him play.
Diehard tackles, rampaging forward,
exhorting teammates, lusting for goals.

I'm double his age, not in his league.
At half-time he's subbed for a while.
Jack says at thirty-two he's lost some pace,
matters more at centre-back
than in midfield: *You just need stamina there.*

A year ago he moved up here,
outsider unsure of getting
in the local team. A year on
he's given teaching the red card,
exhausted by rule changes,

but still chosen by the manager.
I love the touchline accents,
the odd *howay, lad*. Afterwards
the players take down the goalposts
and, like fishermen, gather in the nets.

THE HOMICIDAL CYCLIST

Accidents waited to happen
around every bend. Primitive
suspension, brakes unpredictable.
Mastered the tandem with Jane,
although his own two-wheeler
was another matter.

He ran into a milk cart, ended up
clinging to the head of the pony.
Careered on throughout Surrey,
musing about free love,
bemoaning the invading suburbs,
reconnoitring the territory.

Earmarked localities for destruction.
Rode past Weybridge cricket green,
crossed Walton bridge painted by Canaletto.
Woking was top of his list, his unsuspecting
neighbours destined to expire
in painful and unusual ways.

SOUNDBITE

Your mother brought you back
from the health clinic in high dudgeon.
You hadn't passed the test; they had
marked you down. At the age of two
you knew some words but couldn't
put them together. She sat you
in front of the TV news while she
prepared your dinner. And told you off.

It was only matter of time,
of choosing the right moment,
when it was worth saying something,
something that mattered. Perhaps
the aftermath of some disaster.
Whatever. That was the moment
when you called out to her:
Jack see Mrs Thatcher!

SPIES

They were another tribe
to wary Nether Stowey locals.
Coleridge and his 'Democratic' kind
with their talk of freedom
and The Rights of Man,
their Francophile ways.

That 'hoyden' of a wife sashaying
down the mud-spattered street,
sneered at by shopkeepers.
Friends had letters intercepted
and opened, contents reported
to Whitehall. Revolutionaries.

Amid invasion alerts, and reports
that they had been asking about
a local river and whether it was
navigable from the sea, London's
top spy came down to Stowey
to keep an eye on them.

Dorothy kept in step on their walks,
or a couple behind, dawdling to note down
ideas that William would later seize on.
Sara was generally left at home, managing
wash days, looking after young Hartley,
conjuring up dinner in their hovel.

And the Georgian conspiracy theorists
were right, but not in the way they imagined.
C&W were discussing cultural
revolution, plotting to write poetry
in everyday language, undam a sacred river
of words that common folk could understand.

That gentleman who may have knocked
after trudging over from Porlock
to question an ailing Coleridge –
how could he know or care
if he had unwittingly edited
one of the greatest poems in English literature?

*Acknowledgements to Adam Nicholson's highly recommended
'The Year of Poetry'*

THE OVERMATTER

Borne to the deadline by adrenalin.
While others were out on the town,
you're in the basement; subterranean
intruder, the stone sub-editor,

tolerated by cocky, wisecracking
printers. Every rejigged outcome
a compromise; something
of the night that still crackles

at breakfast. Slash quickly
from the end without recourse
to second thoughts, overmatter
unimportant in the last resort.

Too late for the corrections,
presses ready to roar.
And if this account, smudged and fudged
by jokes, curses, careless typesetters,

falls short of expectations?
Just lead it out, to fill the space.
All the news that fits, to print.

GOODBYE FARRINGDON ROAD

Those Dickensian alleys always suited our sort,
skipping brimming buses, teeming tubes,
coming and going when most people don't.

We'd survived change before; the '88 redesign,
Helvetica bold, like a punch in the face,
three characters shy of a sensitive headline.

Doors kicked in fury, screens left in bits,
drink-sodden casual weeping in the Gents:
Will someone please tell me why I can't get shifts?

Union met in Marx library, or in church crypt.
Time and again they tried it on; for years we
held out, held on to the four-night week.

But new building, new start, they think they've cracked it;
forget circulation in graceful decline,
focus on links, and tags, and hits.

Print's long goodbye, but at what cost?
Farewell Mount Pleasant, Exmouth Market, Farringdon Road;
63's on its way, destination: King's Cross.

*At the end of 2008 the Guardian newspaper relocated its
London offices from Clerkenwell to King's Cross, a terminus
for the 63 bus route, and refocused its priorities, from print to
the internet*

TONGUE TWISTERS

They twist the words from out of your mouth
to fit some wild-eyed, laboured pun
leading a page in the Currant Bun.
Gotta problem? Shut your north and south.
Blokes who stumbled and stammered through school
now speak in tongues all of their own,
language of sex-romps, love-rats, fake-sheikh probes;
lip service to complaints commission rules.

Frenzied buy-ups, celebrity phone-taps,
scoops snatched on doorsteps, red-top tip-offs;
rage and tears at the dying of their day.
Phwoarr! Just take a look at those baps!
Facebook? Twitter? Do you think they're soft?
Screwed up, discarded, the evening giveaways.

SONG OF THE OFSTED INSPECTORS

No point in crying, you know why we're here.
Saw the league tables, smelled blood, descended.
You're on our list; we can wreck your career.

Don't try to fool us; we've been heads, too.
Educating the underclass? A thankless task.
We got out in time, saw which way the wind blew.

Up all night, checking figures? No matter.
We make facts fit, the one thing we're good at.
They all add up, to match the agenda.

The rulers are restless. Times change.
Last year's 'outstanding' is this year's 'good.'
Last year's 'good', we're afraid, is a 'fail.'

Forget paperwork, we've all the answers.
We know you're coasting before we arrive:
it's the new word in the minds of our masters.

A cheerful staffroom? Think you're a success?
We'll take you down a peg or two.
Then splash our findings in the local press.

You know the best thing? No second chances,
no hope of appealing against our verdicts.
We know the truth behind those happy, smiling faces.

THE GAP YEARS
for Kate

At the office I boast of your adventures;
cheering on Chelsea in faraway bars,
trying to ski in the Pyrenees,
taking three trains to Athens at new year,
catching the overnight bus to Madrid.

Driving to Stansted on rain-lashed mornings,
watching for speed traps, the careful parent.
You do those things we should have done
when we were young, but never did;
had you and your brother, I suppose, instead.

The TV that kept switching itself on
in that icy house with the ghost in Osuna.
Searching for the perfect tapas bar.
The bust of Hemingway in Pamplona.
I've read The Sun Also Rises. You lived there.

VALENTINE'S EVE

Took the ferry to Santander,
drove through snow across Iberia,
delivering our daughter's car.

Satnav gave up in Marbella.
We're buggered, you said.
Two near-collisions in the journey's

last moments; realised I'd left
my licence in the kitchen drawer.
The night before was Valentine's Eve:

that moment all the lights came on
in the square at Salamanca.
Crossed the Roman bridge,

saw our breath, lost our bearings.
Too many buildings look
like cathedrals after the Rioja.

EXPATS

After shedding Pennine tears
they fled the rain and men of Yorkshire
to learn the *sevillana*
under Andalusian skies.

Angry and passionate *flamenco*:
the teacher reproved them for smiling.
The four-part *sevillana* was another matter,
something that everyone could master.

Not all Marbella expats sit in beach bars
nursing a beer, a grudge and the Daily Mail.
A blue and white *traje de flamenca*,
spied in a shop window, bought in Madrid,

three *chicas guapas rubias*,
stamping, clapping, spinning,
reminding locals at the feria
just how the dance is done.

SAGRADA FAMILIA

Melting gothic icing; someone
left the cake out in the rain.
Drunk accosts me
at a nearby bar; doesn't want money,
just a quarrel. Laughs at my joke,
accuses me of being American.

Crazy and beautiful Art Nouveau rag.
Poetry readings at El Quatre Gats.
The drunk embraces me roughly,
then squats on the pavement,
tears off his shoe.
Our daughter rushes to pay the bill.

Gaudi was killed by a Barcelona tram.
One day, they say, the cranes will be still.
Stone drips like tears, flows as waves.
Lettering advertises belief on façade.
Overblown, or fabulous homage
to Catalonia? You decide.

O'RAFFERTY'S MOTOR CAR
(*a poem for my granddaughter*)

We used to roar out
the old Val Doonican hit
as we plunged down the street
at full tilt from the pub:
Oh, what a wonderful motor car
It's the greatest ever seen ...
What the residents
of The Roystons in Surbiton
made of our roistering
we didn't linger to find out.

Now I sing the same song
to bemused, two-month-old
Alba in Marbella
in a bid to stop her sobbing.
It used to be black as me father's hat
Now it's forty shades of green ...
I croon at first; then I dance,
wave my arms. Mysterious magic.
After all else fails, her eyelids close.
Little head rests on my shoulder;

I never thought I'd feel this way again.
O Alba, when next we meet
will you still have time
for this old man's tired routine?

ST PETERSBURG

Linger and you're lost. Long after
the revolution has been and gone,
a frenzied mob rackets through the Hermitage,
cramming into the tsar's old quarters,
firing off in all directions, desperately
searching for their leaders among the flags.

Royals gambled with diamonds, serfs remained slaves.
Showy gold leaf of Catherine's summer palace:
despoiled by the Germans during Leningrad's
three-year agony; restored by patriotic
communists. Hired out to ageing
British rockers for birthday bashes.

Late afternoon light on the Neva:
skyline spires across the river,
just as I'd pictured it from tales
of roistering young aristocrats
baiting bemused Pierre
in Tolstoy's War and Peace.

THE ISLANDS OF STOCKHOLM

In the old town
a museum of grandeur:
Einstein, Mandela,
Solzhenitsyn, Mother Teresa.
Nearby hall of fame
for Benny and Frida, Bjorn and Agnetha,
the band that made the world smile,
wearing lurid outfits
with unembarrassed glam swagger.

After grabbing the Eurovision in Brighton,
Abba retreated to the archipelago
to catch their breath,
on the shores, in the woods;
the year I met my wife-to-be.
She swears she doesn't recall this,
doubts that it's true. I thought
they were kinda naff, but still …
The first kiss that started it,
just before her O-levels,
dancing at the party, to Waterloo.

LOIRE

Faraway naked couple
disrupt a crane. It huffs away
as they pursue each other
among terns and cormorants
on a plump sandbank
as wide as a beach.

River invades each winter,
islanders take
to flat-bottomed boats.
But they have standards.
The restaurant-bar where
il n'est pas possible
in the height of summer
just to get a drink.
Quel dommage! we cry forlornly.
Idiotes, the patron mutters,
barely sous his breath.

Indolent islands of the Loire.
Forget Joan of Arc
and the Hundred Years' war.
Plantaganet Angers
is twinned with Wigan.
And Little Weed is really a sunflower.

FINE AND DANDY

Little Plum likes his firewater.
Desperate Dan has diabetes.
Dennis the Menace lived fast,
died young. Walter the Softy
won the Forward prize for poetry.

Hoots! Minnie the Minx
is Scotland's first minister.
Bash Street School's an academy.
Plug lost both legs in Afghanistan.
Teacher leads the Labour party.

Crikey! Snooty shot himself in the foot.
Colonel Blink took over at Ukip.
Oops! Aunt Aggie's
in a care home, her cow pies
banned by health and safety.

Wammo! Beryl the Peril
got a job in Brussels,
Roger couldn't dodge
historic sex offences.
Satire's no laughing matter;
why can't life still be hilarious?

CLACTON
i.m Jox Cox MP

where my brother found a sodden fiver
beside a breakwater and my mother
dried it, spent it on a pair of jeans
for each of us. Riches in those days.
Sealed with A Kiss, Poetry in Motion,
It Might As Well Rain until September
on the jukebox. The train from
Liverpool Street seemed to go on for ever.

Now driving from Clacton through Frinton
to Walton-on-the-Naze past bungalows
with England flags and Vote Leave posters,
bearded old motorbikers roaring through
villages, forests of wind turbines out at sea,
the English in a devil-may-care,
Passport to Pimlico mood.
Give us back our country,

starring those family favourites
Boris Johnson, Michael Gove, Nigel Farage.
As if it were all just an Ealing comedy.

BREXIT BOY

Feels like we've won the league. Yet
I get so angry I want to smash things.
You know that feeling? When people
sneer on the telly, or you talk
to someone who's been to university.
You see their lip curl, when they think
you're not looking. Take back control!

Ain't just the weather, I'm always hot
under the collar. Say what we think
on the buses, down the tube. Tell 'em
to get packing, doesn't matter if they've
lived here years. We took the smirk
off the posh boy's face. Thought
he had it in the bag, didn't he?

Back then you couldn't speak your mind;
now you can shout it out loud.
No one ever asked me what
I thought before. They'd better
not try and twist things round.
Fuck off Europe! Britain will be great again!
First time my vote ever counted for anything.

RETURN OF THE DALEKS

Design classic, some said,
put together when Britain
still had a bit of an empire.
One thought in their heads,
to take over the world.
But inflexible, lacking
imagination, no peripheral
vision, metallic voices.
Hideous inside their boxes,
extremely intolerant
of others not of their kind.

Repeating
the same words
and phrases –
Destroy! Destroy!
Take back control!
Nothing has changed!
- over and over again.
Don't hide behind
the sofa, England!
Come out and push them
down the stairs!

THE MORNING AFTER

the last hope gone, we find ourselves in sunshine
with family in Marbella beside a fountain sculpture
of beauty and unity, reflecting civic pride,
what might have been, playing with our

Anglo-Spanish grandchild on the swings and slides.
She careers across the pavement on a little bike,
I struggle to keep up with her, and as I screw
my features into laughter faces, she mimics every one.

She calls the motorway tunnels along the Costa del Sol
the big dark. That evening the people
of the *barrio* sing carols beneath our flat, with guitars,
harmonies, their brazier a beckoning beacon, bright.

HOW I FAILED TO STOP BREXIT

The year was 2009. I was driving to work
through unsuspecting London streets
one Sunday lunchtime when
the Leader of Her Majesty's Opposition
flagged me down. He and his children
were crossing at traffic lights.

The lights were red; I was braking
but he still felt the need as a parent
to deter me with an imperious
wave of his hand. It was only when I spied
his statuesque wife on the pavement
that I knew the measure of the man.

The incident shook me up as I retold
it at the paper. What if my foot had slipped
on to the accelerator? What if I had
ploughed down the politician
and his children, ruining my own life
as well as ending theirs?

The following year a fruitcake agitator
survived an air crash on election day.
Governing without due care and attention.
Parallel universes, the Highway Code,
a hand of history. With every year,
the route I didn't take mattered

so much more to my country.
End of Stamford street, just
south of Blackfriars bridge, officer.
It's been on my mind a lot lately.

UNHAPPY LANDINGS

Some days he scours the Channel in his boat,
binoculars scanning for hapless migrants
in leaking dinghies; or sits atop
Dover's white cliffs, keeping sentry
on Britain's behalf; or barges into
budget hotels, hunting down those
who have evaded his dragnet;
or wipes away the occasional
milkshake, like seagull poo, that has
landed as if from the sky on his jacket.

Back then he had tottered, shaken,
lucky to be alive, no laughing matter,
from a light aircraft on election day,
the lead item on the first edition story.
By the end of a night when
a divided country had failed
to make up its mind his fall to earth
had been relegated to the last paragraph,
already forgotten, a footnote in history.
Or so it seemed. These days his face,

contorted with fury or snarling laughter,
is everywhere; smirking invader
of our democracy, stirring up
the worst of us with lies and hate,
the man of the people with his pint
of flat beer and friends in the City,
infiltrator disguised as Home Guard,
rabble rouser making mugs of us all.
Yes, he's still a fruitcake: but laughing
at such figures is often a mistake.

REMOANER

He watches TV news
of fishermen netted by lies,
listens to ministers
in rooms brazened with flags,

shakes his head sadly. Waits
in vain for goods ordered
from abroad; wonders
when he will get his jab.

The kind of people who used to say
I'm not being funny but ...
don't feel the same need
to apologise these days.

Donkeys, not lions, he fears,
misled by a clueless clown.
His fading T-shirt
still blue with golden stars.

CLASSIFIEDS

Mature English Blonde lady
offers no-rush massage.
Old postcards wanted
by private collector.
Continence care: bed protection,
pads, briefs, accessories.

Wanted: Dinky toys, model trains.
Underwear by post. Understanding
Attractive Continental lady offers
memorable massage
to discerning gentlemen
in discreet Marylebone surroundings.

Accommodating sensual Japanese lady
offering body to body massage.
Your ancestors found, no task
too big or small. Have you ever
had your wine stock valued?
Memorials to die for.

All old watches and clocks regardless
of condition. Made to measure men's
trousers and plus twos in corduroy,
moleskin and winter tweeds.
Classy Elegant and Friendly Lady,
one minute Sloane Square tube.

*Found poem from adverts in The Oldie Emporium, The Oldie
magazine*

IN BED WITH SID JAMES

I don't know why or when it was
I started laughing like Sid James
in bed. I'd make a risqué joke,
a wisecrack about slap and tickle,
or tackle and suchlike, and his cackle
would come tumbling out,
the yakka-yak-yak
of Hancock's former sidekick.

He was never my Carry On hero.
But when I shouted: *Sid, clear off!*
that was the moment you hated.
That feeling that the South African
comedian, womaniser, gambler
was between the sheets with us.
Or that I'd mistaken
you for Barbara Windsor.

You'd turn away, reach for your tea
and the moment was gone.
I can quite see now
that it wasn't a turn-on.

V

PANTO!

Quick, open the curtains.

What happens next?
What's this scene about?
Will someone keep
those children quiet?

What went wrong there?
Who missed their cue?
Doesn't matter if it goes
tits up, it's only panto,

something to keep out
winter's chill. Forget
what happened
at the dress rehearsal.

The more mistakes
you make, the more the fun.
Dirty jokes, ad-libs a-plenty,
a song and dance or two.

We're missing two pirates.
Has someone seen my
bus conductor's cap?
You can't come in,

the Dame's struggling
into her seventh frock.
O yes I can! Too old for
this game, yet still know how

to play the fool. What if I
forget my lines, the words
don't come? If silence falls,
if there's a pause -

say something

… anything!

THE SHOW

I snapped you on my phone
that Easter Saturday, beside the river,
framed by wisteria, finishing
your Pinot Grigio outside the theatre,

then watched you during the performance
whooping and hollering approval,
bitching and biting your tongue about colleagues,
embracing amigos in the interval.

Tantrums and dressing-downs at rehearsals,
worth it for the dressing-up and laughter.
Cheeky biogs in the programme notes;
surreptitious hugs before you enter.

That's why I'm jealous of your giddy hours;
times when you come alive, the way you glow.
You bask in a sun the rest of us seek,
before, during, after the show.

ALL THE LONELY PEOPLE
Written in response to Sean Henry's sculptures in Woking
town centre

1) Woman (Being Looked At)

All eight foot something and then
some, glowering over shoppers
at the entrance to the mall.
Sideways look, window gazing,
or trying to evade the stares.
Is that a half-smile? Midriff-revealing
top, the shortest of shorts.
Cast work aside, dashed out
in her break. He hasn't shown.
When will she learn?
She feels a fool, so exposed.
Last time she does something like this.
Five minutes longer, no more.
Tries to pretend she's not waiting.
Bit of a Plain Jane, her father once called her,
when he thought she wasn't listening.

2) Standing Man

Perhaps a coffee in the church café
before it closes. Cheap if not cheerful.
Never wanted the job in the first place.
Maybe should have worn a tie?
You always muck it up.
Language, remember where you are.
That woman hanging around
in the precinct, might you

chat her up? Not your type,
too tall, too young. You're no
oil painting, you short-arse,
your glory days long gone.
But still … Forget it, best go home,
get it over with, never grovel,
but don't blurt out the first thing in your head.
Maybe you could write a novel.

3) The Wanderer

I'll always get work. May not
look much but I pack a punch.
The places down this road,
you should see them late.
They spill out into the street.
So, a job on the door.
Hair cut? I like it this way.
This town used to have a reputation.
Less money around, the games they play
on social media. Who knows?
Don't tell me my way of life
is dying. There'll always be fools
out for trouble on a Saturday night.
My hero? Ian Dury, since you ask.
Looked great, and had a way with words.
And Dion and the Belmonts, I suppose.

4) Sleeping Man

Lennon's song on Revolver:
please don't wake him, no, don't shake him …
Did stag-night 'friends' just leave him here?

Comfortable, vulnerable, abandoned.
To sleep, perchance to dream ...
No attribution needed.
Purist, not one for floral patterns;
likes his bedsheets white, pristine.
Hand on the pillow where someone
was just hours, or maybe years ago.
Why did they leave?
Absent, inescapable, still in his head.
Wake up, mate, and smell the coffee!
Duvet day. He is just sleeping, isn't he?
The land of nod. Look, give him a prod.
Every day a lie-in when you're furloughed.

5) Seated Man

Nothing in or out of the station
since God knows when. A jumper
further up the line. Some
commuters tut-tut loudly,
mutter No consideration.
What makes them do it?
It's the drivers you feel sorry for,
need time off to recover.
Time. What does it matter?
If not today, then tomorrow.
All by myself on platform one.
People looking, schoolkids laughing.
A working man with skills no longer wanted.
Tried to keep up appearances, now
I just don't care. Everyone needs a destination.
Makes you want to ... no, don't go there.

YOU REALLY GOT ME

Mated macaws are curious, in that
they mirror each other's behaviour,
being so in love.

It was strange, how it hit me.
You were kneeling on the floor,
intent on solving the Sudoku,
The Kinks playing, old stuff, before your time,
you so focused on the puzzle
yet wiggling your bum to the beat.

And the other funny thing is,
lack of privacy can make a macaw blush.
They blush a lot during the breeding season.

Sometimes I can make you really laugh.
Not always, not often, just sometimes.
Then your faces crinkles up.
And your eyes, they're so happy.
And your eyes, well, they dance.

THE MERMAID'S PURSE

Traffic-trapped near Bristol I let loose
Hughes on the CD player. His voice
haunting, hypnotic, knife-like
distracted me from gridlock.
You suffered in silence
for as long as you could.

Reached the Worm's Head mid-evening,
where Dylan Thomas was stranded
by the tide. Beachcombing next morning,
you showed me mermaids purses
strewn along the strand, egg
pouches of shark and skate.

Bones of a shipwreck poked through
Rhossili's sand. What would Plath
have made of this? That night,
unforgettable birthday party in full swing,
we slouched in old sofas
around the bonfire on the clifftop,

watching shooting stars dash through the heavens
for the first time in our lives.

BRUGES

Your imagination is captured
by a beguinage in Bruges;
enclosed residence
for unmarried or widowed
women who adopt
a life of religious devotion,
without taking a nun's full vows.
They live in solitude,
in small, separate houses.
How wonderful, you say.
A life without men. No snoring,
or having to watch Match of the Day.

Our boatman appears to be British,
pukka accent, sense of humour,
snobbish about architecture.
Safe hands. But references
to "blinking" and Blighty
give him away. Language
of war comics; more English
than the English. Public art:
four horsemen's black humour;
out-of-control pony and tourist,
trapped. Shop name
to remember: the Chocolate Kiss.

We only heard the coast was clear
an hour before departure,
your father safely through
his operation. Hooves echoed
on the cobbles; evening bell,
the closing of the gates.
Lingered over one more Trappist
beer, misread the train ticket.
Climbed 300-odd steps
of the tower, thinking
it could be the last time
we do something like this.

THE FLICKERING STARS

The beginning of another evening
when you're not going out.
The time of day when you need a drink.

From five, sometimes earlier,
I watch Brando, Bogart;
On The Waterfront, The Big Sleep.

But just before bedtime, if the
weather permits, I go to the patio,
sit for a few moments in the dark,

gaze at stars flickering in the heavens,
hear the comfort of an owl's hoot.

A LONG WAY FROM THE FRONT LINE

Disposable gloves
in the glove compartment.

Sparrows chatter in the bamboo
as we sip prosecco on the patio
and talk about changing our wills.

The interminable thump
of ball against wall.

I have cosseted that clematis
outside the kitchen window
with water and teabags.
Now the buds are ready
to burst open like teardrops.

But every Thursday evening at eight
we stand outside our front doors
and clap, and maybe holler, too,
and try to imagine for a moment
what it's like, in their shoes, in ICU.

VE DAY ANNIVERSARY

A minute's silence
among tomatoes, baked beans.
Brush away a tear.

An old song's moment,
broadcast in the superstore.
We *will* meet again.

THURSDAY

The elder of the two little girls
next door stands on the
cherry tree stump to clap.

They're not due
back to school yet.
We chat, have our weekly

catch-up with people who after
all these years we've only
just got to know. And you

can't help wondering,
how much longer
will we keep all this up?

OUR AMY

That holiday in Anglesey
playing her hit CD in the car,
I didn't really get her.
Menai bridge, choughs
at South Stack, we joined
the RSPB, the little railway
into Snowdonia, the washing line
like a deranged turbine in the gales.

Then watching last night on TV
the illegal parties broken up
by police, beaches trashed,
a nod and a wink, the end
of hibernation for bears
that shit under the pier.
The beasts, and the beauty.
Amy in her prime at Glastonbury

singing in the rain, hitching
up her trousers, tottering
off stage briefly in her heels,
earnest schoolgirl
hardly ever smiling,
impossible beehive,
famine-victim limbs,
the boyfriend watching

from the wings, hunted down
by tabloids, and through
it all her sublime, seemingly
effortless drawl that makes us
sigh with pleasure and loss.
Nation's sweetheart. Our Amy.
All those classic torch songs
she could have made her own.

FRAN AND THE ELEPHANT

His mother croons.
He tries to smile,
kicks his legs,
grips a toy elephant,
tries to say *Elephant*,
sing a song.
He is puzzled and cheerful
and patient. He knows
that all these things will come.

V

THE JAB

Signs tied to lampposts point
the way from the free car park,
past ambulance waiting discreetly,
help you to find the place easily.
Legions of people in hi-vis jackets
with nice, kind smiles bustle
about, wipe tables and chairs,
give you a number, tell you
where to sit. You discover
you're getting the 'right' one,
much to your relief. And at some

moment when you're not expecting
it, just sitting there, watching
the busying volunteers
you well up, you can't help it,
tears spring to your eyes,
it takes you by surprise, thinking
about all that's happened,
the long months that have come
to this. People working together
for the greater good. Our NHS.
This side-effect is common, I believe.

'LOVE MAKES YOU RECKLESS'

Grandchildren in another country, growing up on Facetime
before our eyes. Joy of a family Sunday lunch
in Benahavis, lockdown blurted out after we flew to Spain,
my determined wife vetoing my fears, I wondering when
or if we might ever go home. Love makes you reckless.

Full moon at Halloween. Sitting on Kate and Juan's patio,
looking across the valley to the hill and mountain beyond,
thinking absurdly of my own grandmother's tiny
back garden terrace close to the Kingston by-pass,
where I always felt nothing but love.

The cactus, the palm, and the orange chrysanthemum
blooming brightly in November. *La Concha* mountain
spreads its limbs almost to the shore.
On San Pedro's *paseo* I remove my mask,
and for the first time smell the sea.